A Practical Guide to Teaching Gymnastics

ISBN: 978-1-905540-38-9

Authors: Barry Benn, Tansin Benn and Patricia Maude

Project lead officer: Sue Wilkinson

Coachwise editorial and design team: Lucy Histed, Matthew Dodd and Samantha Wiggle

Filming, DVD design and production by Steve Cridge.
Voice-over by Patricia Maude.

The Association for Physical Education (afPE) is the physical education subject association for all professionals with appropriate qualifications in physical education, sport and dance.

Photos © afPE unless otherwise stated

With special thanks and acknowledgement to the following teachers and their pupils: Laura Brownhill, Paul Bryant, Richard Grainger, Roger Lilley, Belinda Samuels, Penny Speer and Karen Watson; all who participated in the filming at Baverstock Specialist Sports College, Birmingham; Hills Road VI Form College, Cambridge; King Edward School, Birmingham; Milton Road Primary School, Cambridge; Morley Memorial Primary School, Cambridge; Netherhall Specialist Sports College, Cambridge; William Westley CE Primary School, Whittlesford, Cambridge; the following coaches and their gymnasts: Lisa Higgins, Chris Panter and Mary Small, and Baverstock School Gymnastics Club, City of Birmingham Gymnastics Club, Homerton Gymnastics Club, Cambridge, and West Bromwich Gymnastics Club.

This publication represents well-intended guidance. It is assumed that appropriate risk assessment will be undertaken in connection with all the activity described in the text.

association for
Physical Education

Room SC26
University of Worcester
Henwick Grove
Worcester
WR2 6AJ
Tel: 01905-855 584
Fax: 01905-855 594

Building 25
London Road
Reading
RG1 5AQ
Tel: 0118-378 6240
Fax: 0118-378 6242

Email: enquiries@afpe.org.uk Website: www.afpe.org.uk

Published on behalf of afPE by

Coachwise

Coachwise Limited
Chelsea Close
Off Amberley Road
Armley
Leeds LS12 4HP

Tel: 0113-231 1310 Fax: 0113-231 9606
Email: enquiries@coachwise.ltd.uk
Website: www.coachwise.ltd.uk

060273

Contents

Introduction   **1**

Gymnastics at Key Stages 2 and 3   2

Structure and Use of the Resource   2

Section 1: Synopses of Units of Work   **5**

Unit 1 – Year 4 (P1)   6

Unit 2 – Year 6 (P2)   8

Unit 3 – Year 7 (S1)   10

Unit 4 – Year 8 (S2)   12

Section 2: Dimensions of Learning through Gymnastics   **15**

Dimension 1: Facilitating Learning   15

Dimension 2: Acquiring and Developing Skills   17

Dimension 3: Composition   21

Dimension 4: Assessment for Learning   25

Dimension 5: Extending Learning – School Sport–Club Links   27

Dimension 6: Knowledge of Health and Fitness   31

Dimension 7: Lifelong Learning   33

Section 3: Additional Resources   **37**

Glossary   37

Skill-ladder Charts   39

Balance Charts   45

Physical Preparation Chart   47

User Notes for the DVD and DVD-ROM   48

Foreword

This is the second resource in the Practical Guide to Teaching series, which responds to teachers' need for guidance that is grounded in school practice but is technically well informed and structured. Gymnastics is at the heart of physical education, providing the fundamental skills of body management, which are the basis for all children to become effective movers. Gymnastic activities are also a statutory programme of study in National Curriculum Physical Education. Best of all, gymnastics offers controlled excitement and the sheer joy of movement: in gymnastics, the body and its movement are the medium of learning, performance and achievement.

Yet, for many teachers, teaching gymnastics can be challenging, partly because of the perceived risk, but also because they may not have had the benefit of adequate initial teacher training in gymnastics and thus lack the confidence, skills or knowledge to make a start. In some cases, teachers are confident enough to make a start, but are less certain about how to increase challenge and achieve progression, especially for children who are more experienced gymnasts.

A Practical Guide to Teaching Gymnastics is intended to support teachers working with children aged 7–14 years, and to facilitate school and community club links. The resource provides accessible help, with plenty of concrete ideas, aiming to build confidence, and extend knowledge, skills and understanding of learning and teaching in and through gymnastics.

The authors, all well respected teachers and coaches of gymnastics for the whole age range of school children, offer a wealth of experience and a reservoir of ideas, which teachers can use to ensure that children enjoy the mastery, achievement and richness of gymnastics.

The Association for Physical Education and British Gymnastics are delighted to jointly commend this resource.

Margaret Talbot
Chief Executive, The Association
for Physical Education

Alan Somerville
Chief Executive, British
Gymnastics

About the Authors

Each of the three authors has experience that spans over 30 years of professional contribution to learning, teaching, coaching and development of gymnastics across education and community provision.

After training at Loughborough, **Barry Benn** (MA) taught in the secondary, primary and adult education sectors before becoming the Gymnastics Development Officer for the City of Birmingham. After a successful competitive career, Barry coached gymnasts, both men and women, to international level, receiving Honorary National Coach status in 1975 and the Long Service Award of the Association of British Gymnastic Coaches in 1991. Barry also served as an international judge of Men's Artistic Gymnastics for over 25 years and was a member of several national technical committees for British Gymnastics and the British Schools' Gymnastics Association. He has authored many texts related to teaching gymnastics and, recently, on sociological analysis of the sport of gymnastics. Barry is currently lecturing in physical education and sport in the School of Education at the University of Birmingham.

Dr Tansin Benn is currently Associate Professor in the School of Education at the University of Birmingham. Starting her career as a Physical Education teacher, Tansin moved into teacher training at both primary and secondary levels and, later, into wider university contributions, including management and research. She worked voluntarily in the sport of Women's Artistic Gymnastics, as a coach and international judge, as well as serving on regional and national technical committees to assist the development, organisation and management of the sport. Tansin has authored books and journal articles on theory and practice related to the field, most recently, in sociological analysis of developments in the sport of gymnastics.

Patricia Maude was awarded an MBE for services to physical education in 2001. Formerly a full-time principal lecturer in teacher education at Homerton College, University of Cambridge, she is now a part-time tutor and physical education consultant. Patricia has completed extensive research into movement development for young children and has contributed regionally and nationally as adviser, author, coach, judge and tutor for British Gymnastics. Her major contribution has been in general gymnastics and teacher/tutor training. Patricia's leading-edge contributions to interactive resource materials for teachers have included *Observing Children Moving* (2003) and *Observing and Analysing Learners' Movement* (2006).

Introduction

A Practical Guide to Teaching Gymnastics is a unique and comprehensive interactive resource, made up of a handbook and a DVD/DVD-ROM, which illustrates aspects of continuity and progression in primary and secondary schools and club gymnastics. This resource has been designed to contribute to the delivery of high-quality curriculum gymnastics experiences, leading to the raising of standards for pupils, particularly in the age range of between 7 and 14 years. The resource is in line with the school–club links strand, which is promoted in the national Physical Education, School Sport and Club Links (PESSCL) Strategy in England.

Inspiration for the aesthetic and creative potential of gymnastic activity and the intrinsic motivation that drives performers can be seen in the exceptional movement mastery, versatility, creativity, control and precision of gymnasts in Cirque du Soleil or Parkour (illustrated below) performances. Immediacy of appreciation for the daring, courage and management of risk is captured in 'breath-holding' moments of exhilaration when performers seem to defy gravity in spectacular ways.

Gymnastics can make a unique contribution to lifelong learning. It also contributes to a balanced physical education and to the goal of gaining physical literacy. In the gymnastics context, pupils can experience developmental movement mastery; the discipline of refining skills and sequences to optimise performance; precision, creativity and interpretation in movement; and the use of apparatus in ever-increasingly challenging and complex ways. Working at appropriate, differentiated levels, pupils acquire knowledge, skills and understanding through gymnastics and experience satisfaction by achieving success.

A key objective of this pedagogical resource is to focus on the contribution trainees, teachers, coaches and other professionals can make to pupils' learning through gymnastics. Incremental learning, progress and achievement are central concepts exemplified throughout the resource.

1

Gymnastics at Key Stages 2 and 3 (7–14 Years)

Prior to Key Stage 2 (aged 7 years), pupils have begun to acquire and develop a gymnastics-specific **movement vocabulary of actions and skills** on both the floor and apparatus. They have gained experience in selecting from that vocabulary actions and skills to build **gymnastics phrases and sequences** and thereby develop their creative skills and movement memory. Opportunities to **evaluate their own work and the work of others**, through seeing, describing, analysing and giving feedback, are often presented. These aspects enable pupils to begin to understand ways of achieving **movement quality** in their gymnastics.

Learning in Key Stages 2 and 3 (aged 7–14 years) should build on pupils' previous experience. This enables all learners to continue to extend their movement vocabulary and skills-learning, broaden their knowledge and understanding, develop creativity to structure and perform more complex sequences and engage in more critical reflection on their own and others' performances.

The need for strength and suppleness in the performance of a range of gymnastic skills ensures a focus on these two aspects of health and fitness in a practical, applied situation. Also, knowledge and understanding of cardio-respiratory fitness can be developed in the physical-preparation games and activities, which are designed to improve agility and stamina in gymnastics.

The national curriculum in England entitles every child to be physically educated. School is the only environment in which every child can engage in a gymnastics learning experience. The international gymnasts of the future are currently present in our education system. Teachers and coaches working in schools have a responsibility to identify the needs and potential of their pupils in physical activity. These influential people need to understand generic movement education, to be aware of the early stages of the Long-term Athlete Development programme and sport-specific training opportunities, and to cater for pupils who are Gifted and Talented in physical education and school sport.

Structure and Use of the Resource

A Practical Guide to Teaching Gymnastics is made up of a handbook and a DVD/DVD-ROM. To make the most of this resource, it is recommended that users select a Unit or a Dimension and work systematically through the pre-viewing, video extracts, extension material and follow-up activities/tasks, according to the icons illustrated (as shown on the opposite page).

The Handbook

The handbook is made up of three sections, each of which links directly to, and is integrated with, the video extracts on the DVD. The handbook and DVD are designed to be used alongside one another.

Section 1: Synopses of Units of Work

Each unit synopsis contains overviews of lesson structures, content in practice and unit progressions, rather than demonstrating a single lesson. Information on the number and length of the lessons can be found at the start of each unit. The four units are:

- Unit 1 – (**P1**) Primary school (Year 4, pupils aged 8–9 years)
- Unit 2 – (**P2**) Primary school (Year 6, pupils aged 10–11 years)
- Unit 3 – (**S1**) Secondary school (Year 7, pupils aged 11–12 years)
- Unit 4 – (**S2**) Secondary school (Year 8, pupils aged 13–14 years).

The codes P1, P2, S1 and S2 refer throughout the handbook and on the DVD to the four classes of pupils.

Section 2: Dimensions of Learning through Gymnastics

In this section of the handbook, you will find seven dimensions of learning and teaching through gymnastics. These include aspects of pedagogy, content and progression in the gymnastics curriculum and club development, culminating in consideration of lifelong learning. In summary, these dimensions are:

1. Facilitating Learning
2. Acquiring and Developing Skills
3. Composition
4. Assessment for Learning
5. Extending Learning – School Sport/Club Links
6. Knowledge of Health and Fitness
7. Lifelong Learning.

To assist with navigation, there are four icons, which indicate:

 pre-viewing information that provides guidance on the content of the DVD

 video extracts on the DVD to be viewed

 extension material providing additional information about each dimension

 suggested **follow-up activities/tasks**.

Section 3: Additional Resources

The Skill-ladder, Physical Preparation and Partner and Group Balance **Charts** provide visual resources for teachers and pupils to extend learning as appropriate and can be photocopied.

The **Glossary** provides definitions of terms and concepts as they are to be interpreted for use in this resource.

The DVD

 **Section 1: Video Extracts of Unit Synopses**

These video extracts are intended to act as a stimulus to encourage the viewer to consider

aspects of high-quality teaching and learning. The sequence of the four units is intended to promote consideration of continuity and progression in learning, across the stages of the education process:

- Unit 1 – (**P1**) Primary school (Year 4, pupils aged 8–9 years)
- Unit 2 – (**P2**) Primary school (Year 6, pupils aged 10–11 years)
- Unit 3 – (**S1**) Secondary school (Year 7, pupils aged 11–12 years)
- Unit 4 – (**S2**) Secondary school (Year 8, pupils aged 13–14 years).
- School Clubs (**SC**)

The codes P1, P2, S1 and S2 refer throughout the handbook and on the DVD to the four classes of pupils shown on the DVD.

Section 2: Dimensions of Learning Exemplified through Gymnastics

The second section of the DVD is made up of five of the seven dimensions, namely:

1 Facilitating Learning

2 Acquiring and Developing Skills

3 Composition

4 Assessment for Learning

5 Extending Learning – School Sport–Club Links.

Gymnastics in action is shown by means of a series of short video extracts and still image montages, selected to exemplify the constituent segments of each dimension. The DVD includes video extracts of teachers and learners working in a range of settings, using a variety of resources appropriate for gymnastics in both curriculum and club sessions. The gymnastics club work illustrated is from school clubs and local community gymnastic centres.

DVD-ROM

On the DVD-ROM, you will find the following reference material and resources for use by teachers and pupils:

- An introduction to the contents of the DVD-ROM
- **Folder 1**
  - Movement Analysis Worksheet – Examples of Gymnastic Action Categories
  - Movement Analysis Worksheet – Ways of Varying Gymnastic Actions
  - Pupil Self-assessment and Gymnastics Vocabulary Record
  - An Example of a Completed Pupil Self-assessment and Gymnastics Vocabulary Record

3

© www.actionplus.co.uk

- Sequence-building Worksheet
- An Example of a completed Sequence-building Worksheet
- Pupil Self-assessment Worksheet 1
- Example of a Completed Pupil Self-assessment Worksheet 1
- Pupil Self-assessment Worksheet 2
- Example of a Completed Pupil Self-assessment Worksheet 2

- **Folder 2**
  - Dimensions of Learning
  - Sample Skill-ladder Charts
  - Sample Partner and Group Balance Charts
  - Sample Physical Preparation Chart

- **Folder 3**
  - References and Further Resources
    British Gymnastics Resources and Courses

The References section provides web links, and details of published material from afPE, British Gymnastics and other sources.

The material illustrated in the resource is part of ongoing curriculum and club gymnastics in the situations shown. Teachers and coaches using the resource are encouraged to select ideas and material suitable for their own schools and clubs, knowledge level, pupils' needs and background experience, and local authority context.

Section 1: Synopses of Units of Work

The Unit Synopses (P1, P2, S1 and S2), illustrated by the video extracts on the DVD, show lesson development and unit progression, rather than being a representation of a single lesson. In this way, it has been possible to select from a wide variety of examples to show skill acquisition, sequence development, learning and teaching about assessment, and consideration of the contributions gymnastics can make to fitness and health. Time is needed for pupils to develop knowledge, skills and understanding at each stage of learning, to ensure high-quality success and to challenge them through gymnastic activity. Progress is always dependent on the specific situation, background experience and individual needs.

5

Unit 1 – Year 4 (P1)

This unit was taught over six weeks with two lessons of an hour each week, using material drawn from the local authority gymnastics scheme (Cambridgeshire Scheme of Work for Physical Education).

Core Aim

The core aim is for pupils to increase their knowledge, skills and understanding of the gymnastic actions, techniques and progressions related to rotation. They work towards performing short individual sequences of two rotations with a link, on the floor and apparatus. Peer mentoring is developed to increase the pupils' ability to observe, describe in gymnastics vocabulary and make formative assessments. As this was the first term in the new school building, the pupils also learned how to manage the new apparatus.

Learning Objectives	Outcomes/Evidence
The objectives are for the pupils to:	By the end of the unit, the pupils should be able to:
learn about and perform a range of rotational actions, focusing on correct alignment, body tension and control, and be able to describe them	describe and perform a variety of rotations, including roll, spin, turn and twist
plan and perform sequences using different rotational actions	select two rotations and link them into a sequence
cooperate with others in setting up, using, dismantling and storing apparatus	carry and set up apparatus appropriately with others; work on the full range of apparatus and put it away
observe and describe the performances of others, focusing on quality.	observe a partner closely, then talk about and demonstrate achievements and areas for development.

Introduction and Physical Preparation

Questioning by the teacher is used, often in the classroom, to remind pupils of the core aim of the work. This facilitates recall, focuses them on gymnastics and enables review of the technical terms to be used. Exemplified in the DVD are named travelling actions, including 'skip', 'chassé', 'gallop' and the 'gymnastic walk'. This latter action was being used throughout the school to help the pupils to concentrate on posture and extended body shape. In several lessons, travelling and rotating activities formed part of the introductory, cardio-respiratory and movement vocabulary work. The pupils work alone and are encouraged to use all the space and vary their direction of travel.

'Conditioned phrases' are physical preparation sequences, introduced and developed in each lesson of every unit throughout the school. These provide pupils with movement vocabulary, appropriate for the core tasks of the unit, in this case, to develop rotation in gymnastics. One or two elements are introduced in the first lessons of a unit and the sequence is lengthened as the unit progresses. This gradual extension of the sequence also helps to develop the pupils' movement memory. The sequence shown includes:

- a circle roll (sideways from sitting in straddle shape)
- a log roll (straight)
- an egg roll (tucked)
- rocking (on the back to stand up)
- a twist at the end.

The pupils recall the names of the actions in their order in the sequence before starting. These actions can then be applied as needed in subsequent mat and apparatus work and pupils are also encouraged to explore other related movement vocabulary. Peer observation, analysis and feedback feature as part of the assessment for learning in every lesson. Pupils tell their partner the features of good quality that they see and also demonstrate ways of improving performance. The teacher helps the pupils to identify focal points, such as 'extending ankles and pointy toes' and 'working with control'.

Development

1 Floor work – As the floor sequences include work on the forward roll, for which, at this stage in their learning, the pupils need mats, they next carry and set out the mats. Peer mentoring continues as they work on their rolls and other rotation actions. Use of demonstration enables everyone to focus on the task and to remember that short sequences are required. After several weeks, the mat work will culminate in demonstrations of short, complete sequences of two linked rotations, with a start and finish. The teacher gives feedback and support to pupils as they work and discusses their sequences, encouraging them to explain and demonstrate their work.

2 Apparatus work – As this was the first term in the new school building, apparatus work offered opportunities for the pupils, during each lesson, to become familiar with the apparatus plan. They did this through learning how to cooperate in setting up and dismantling the apparatus themselves. The teacher checked that the apparatus was correctly set up and spaced appropriately. The pupils then explored the potential of each piece, in order to start building a working movement vocabulary of rotations, along with travelling from one piece of apparatus to another. Time was spent practising ways of getting onto and off apparatus, in order to ensure that they could access each piece. This also provided variety in subsequent lessons when a core task would be to create apparatus sequences.

Conclusion

The school adopts a variety of ways of ending lessons, including class, peer and group discussion and feedback. The video example is of several pupils explaining what they have learnt.

View video extract Unit 1 (P1).

The following suggested follow-up activities/tasks can be used with any of the four units (P1, P2, S1 and S2).

1 From the material illustrated in the Unit, plan a series of six lessons, each of 45 minutes, to show progression in learning.

2 With a focus on learning in and through gymnastics, identify learning that could precede and follow the unit illustrated.

Unit 2 – Year 6 (P2)

 This unit was taught over six weeks with two lessons of an hour each week, using material drawn from the local authority gymnastics scheme (Cambridgeshire Scheme of Work for Physical Education).

Core Aim

The aim is for pupils to increase their knowledge, skills and understanding of body conditioning for gymnastics and to work cooperatively to develop fluent sequences with a partner. Development includes making and negotiating bridges and balances in both floor work and on the new apparatus.

Learning Objectives	Outcomes/Evidence
The objectives are for the pupils to:	By the end of the unit, the pupils should be able to:
understand the importance of physical preparation, through performing conditioning phrases with increasing demands on body tension	respond to related questions and perform conditioned phrases accurately, with appropriate body tension and precise body shape
create and hold balances and bridge shapes as obstacles, using a variety of body parts	perform floor sequences with a partner and group, including travelling over, under, around and through bridge shapes and balances
focus on transitions in sequences, to achieve greater continuity and fluency	demonstrate smooth, continuous and fluent transitions and be able to describe how these are achieved
develop sequences with a partner on the variety of apparatus in the new hall	practise on the full range of apparatus and perform partner sequences, negotiating bridges and balances performed on the apparatus
observe and make formative assessments of others, focusing on composition and fluency of movement.	accurately describe the quality of both the actions in sequences and the fluency of transitions between actions.

Introduction and Physical Preparation

Introductions to lessons and the setting of the learning objective and first task sometimes occur in the classroom. This ensures that the pupils are active as soon as they enter the hall. On the video extract, the teacher introduces the session in the hall for the benefit of the viewers of the DVD. The learning objective is established through teacher questioning. The first activity then enables the pupils to concentrate on bridging and balancing in pairs, with 'lead and follow travelling' as a contrasting activity.

'Conditioned phrases' are physical preparation sequences, introduced and developed in each lesson of the unit. These provide pupils with movement vocabulary, appropriate for the core tasks of the unit, and also help them to learn more about physical preparation (including the development of strength and flexibility) in order to improve their body condition and gymnastic performance.

The conditioned phrase exemplified on the DVD focuses on balances that are also 'bridges', along with resilient and fluent transitions between them. These include postural control at the start, balancing on the balls of the feet, and moving through a bridge shape into front support and then back support. These activities help develop core stability. The phrase also includes a shoulder balance and a bridge or crab. The initial conditioned phrase in a unit is suggested by the teacher. Later, pupils are tasked to develop this in a variety of ways. These include:

- peer mentoring the given phrase
- creating their own conditioned phrases in line with the core task
- sharing these conditioned phrases and teaching them to others
- videoing each others' work for peer assessment
- using conditioned phrases to learn more about strategies in assessment for learning
- recording conditioned phrases as part of their record of achievement.

Development

1 Floor work – The example included on the DVD video shows the development of the conditioned phrase through partner work. One pupil works on improving the shape and control of the bridges and balances in the conditioned phrase, holding each for the other pupil to negotiate, by going over, under, around or through. The pupils decide when to change roles. In this way, pupils also practise a wider range of movement vocabulary, including jumping and landing, rolling, inversion, and stepping, as well as balancing. The task of improving fluency is particularly challenging for the pupil who is

negotiating, in order to ensure that the end of one action is linked directly to the next. As the pupils become more familiar with their partner's balances and bridges, the transitions improve in fluency of action, direction, variety, resilience and control. An example of half-class observation, assessment and feedback is shown in the DVD video extracts.

The pupils also gain experience of working in larger groups. Working with others whom they know is a valuable experience in the final year of primary school, prior to transferring to secondary school and developing group cooperation skills with new peers.

2 Apparatus work – The pupils assemble the fixed apparatus, the large and small portable apparatus and then place the mats with the apparent ease that comes from experience and maturity. At this stage in their learning, they have developed ideas for using the apparatus, mats and floor to create a variety of balances and bridges, working alone and travelling freely from one apparatus to another. They are encouraged to include some work that is entirely on apparatus and some that is partly on apparatus and partly on mats or the floor. Working in pairs offers a greater challenge and great care is taken to negotiate partners on apparatus with precision and sensitivity. In subsequent lessons, pupils were tasked to create and perform partner and group sequences on the apparatus.

Conclusion

After putting away the apparatus, the teacher leads a class discussion and prompts the pupils to evaluate their learning critically. Pupils report that they have learnt:

- that balances need not always be static
- to work to achieve silent landings
- the importance of body tension
- to improve the fluency of transitions in their sequences
- to control each part of a sequence
- to include contrasts between partners in sequences.

The teacher follows up with a further probing question about types of contrast. The pupils include levels, speeds, body shapes and use of symmetry and asymmetry in their responses. Following the session, several pupils talk further about their learning.

 View video extract Unit 2 (P2).

 For suggested follow-up tasks, see page 7.

Unit 3 – Year 7 (S1)

 This unit was taught over 12 lessons, lasting 45 minutes each.

Core Aim

The aim is for pupils to increase their knowledge, skills and understanding of selected inversion and travelling gymnastic skills techniques and progressions, working towards individual sequences that show variations in shape. Peer mentoring is used at each stage of the unit.

Learning Objectives	Outcomes/Evidence
The objectives are for the pupils to:	By the end of the unit, the pupils should be able to:
understand the importance of physical preparation, techniques of specific skills and levels of progression in skill-learning	respond to related questions, demonstrate selection and use of appropriate skill progression levels, and apply criteria in peer mentoring situations
use variations into and out of skills to develop sequences using the floor and apparatus	perform an individual sequence with control, using a variety of ways into and out of skills (eg turn, twist, step, change of shape and direction)
apply the concepts of shape and direction to sequence development	demonstrate varied use of shape and direction in sequences and recognise these spatial concepts in the work of others
engage in peer mentoring to improve the performance of a partner.	communicate constructively to a partner, applying knowledge and understanding through observation and feedback, using technical and compositional criteria, to make a positive difference.

Introduction and Physical Preparation

In the introduction to the lesson on the DVD, pupils are shown performing continuous relays to ensure vigorous and purposeful activity. Each week new movement challenges are added (eg running straight, running around or between others, different types of jumping, such as hopping and leaping). These lengthen the continuous relays, thereby developing movement memory and increasing cardio-respiratory demands.

Physical preparation continues weekly, with exercises to help build strength and suppleness. The example on the DVD shows the development of a movement phrase across a number of lessons, built on sustaining a front support position to improve the centre body tension. Interest is sustained and the physical demands are gradually increased by adding extra exercises week by week. This also serves to develop movement memory. The additional exercises could be suggested by the teacher and/or pupils.

Development

The development section of lessons focuses on the main core of the unit and involves concentrated time on learning through skill development and sequencing.

1 Skill development – Early lessons focus on giving pupils time to use the Skill-ladder Charts to explore the progressions shown, in order to identify their personal level for high-quality performance. They use the charts and apparatus to explore, practise and refine their work. The visual aids are a constant point of reference and reinforcement for learning. Activities illustrated range from simple to complex and also provide diverse apparatus situations in which the actions can be improved and practised safely. The emphasis for this stage of the unit is on quality so, in the example shown on the DVD, the boys had to make judgements about their own performance level and rate of progress up the ladder, what they could do and what they would like to try. The pupils learn to assess their abilities, make decisions for themselves, and evaluate and improve their performance against technical points and images shown on the chart.

2 Sequence development – Once skill levels have been identified and practised, each pupil can progress to linking these into an individual sequence. Pupils start with finding different ways into and out of the skill level, using a range of ideas (such as changing the direction or shape, moving into another action, or using linking movements like steps and turns). From here, they progress to sequence

development, which includes their selected skills and clear changes of shape and direction. When observing each other's work, the pupils were asked to identify positive aspects of each performance; they answered:

- control
- good linking movements
- clear start and end
- 'I liked George's because…'.

They also provided constructive criticism, identifying the need:

- to improve 'floppy legs'
- for more body tension and extension
- for attention to some of the technical points shown on the charts.

Conclusion

There are many ways to finish a lesson; for example, gradually slowing the activity demands and pace after vigorous exercise, reinforcing and reflecting on learning, and ensuring continuity of understanding across weekly lessons and throughout the progression of the term. The video example shows the teacher reviewing pupils' learning at the end of their unit. The pupils' comments included the following:

- 'It doesn't matter if you are good or bad, you can work at your own level – with quality.'
- 'It takes time and practice to become a good gymnast.'
- 'If you see something that can be improved, you can help someone else.'
- 'When we started gymnastics I was no good at it, now I am good at it.'

The final video extract shows the teacher reviewing an individual pupil's understanding of the school assessment system, which steers their progress and targets and monitors achievements. The synopsis closes with the teacher's overview.

 View video extract Unit 3 (S1).

 For suggested follow-up tasks, see page 7.

Unit 4 – Year 8 (S2)

This unit was taught for six weeks, through a one-hour lesson each week.

Core Aim

The aim is for pupils to increase their knowledge, skills and understanding through group work, focusing on developing collaborative balances and linking these into sequences, showing an interesting use of pathways.

Learning Objectives	Outcomes/Evidence
The objectives for the pupils are to:	By the end of the unit, the pupils should be able to:
understand the principles of safe weight-bearing when balancing in groups and the importance of strength and body tension	demonstrate knowledge and understanding through responses to questions, application in performance and safe execution of physical preparation and skills development
cooperate to develop a range of group balances on the floor and apparatus	contribute creative ideas and assume responsibility for collaborative skill development
work into and out of group balances, using interesting pathways	share in problem-solving and decision-making, and in giving and receiving ideas
create a sequence by connecting group balances on the floor and apparatus, using interesting pathways	engage in the process of sequence development from exploration to performance
provide constructive critical evaluation of their own work and that of others.	justify responses in terms of task parameters and appropriate criteria for value judgements made.

Introduction and Physical Preparation

The video extract begins with the teacher leading pupils in an aerobics warm-up routine, which has been developed week by week. This develops physical demands gradually and introduces the use of music, which floor groups could later use in sequencing. Music adds a motivational dimension to learning, helping pupils with musicality, rhythm and phrasing. Physical preparation continues with three body tension exercises to strengthen and increase awareness of particular muscle groups essential to later skills work.

Development

1 Floor work: Pairs balancing – In the development part of each lesson, the pupils work towards the goal of group sequencing on the floor and apparatus, using interesting pathways. They start with partner balancing, using the Pairs Balance Chart as a stimulus for their initial ideas. The charts also give important safety points, for example, about body alignment, which are reinforced by the teacher. Technical points, such as the mechanical principles of weight-bearing, structures, grips and supports, are introduced. Pupils explore these and their own ideas, often with the help of a third 'critical friend' to offer support, advice and confidence. The teacher provides constant reinforcement about safety and the responsibilities of both base (person supporting) and top (person being balanced). When questioned on safety, the pupils in the example on the DVD identified the need:

- for a strong base
- for the top to have good body tension
- to keep legs and arms straight for support
- for the weight to be spread over a strong support
- to look for vertical, straight body lines when taking weight
- to recognise that 'it's OK to help each other into and out of balances'.

These answers stimulated ideas that could then be developed into partner sequences, showing two of their favourite balances and interesting and different floor patterns to connect them. The more creative the task, the more time the pupils need for negotiation, discussion, exploration, trial and error in the search for their own resolutions.

2 Group balancing and sequencing – Once familiar with the basic principles and concepts, the next stage of the unit involves group work, on both the floor and apparatus. The Group Balance Chart is used to offer starter ideas. The pupils can use this flexibly and make their own choices and adaptations, as well as develop their own material. Again, more time is needed for groups to engage in

the processes of negotiation, problem-solving, decision-making and exploration. Floor groups have the added challenge and motivation of working to music for their sequences. The complexity of working in groups means that communication is often easier using musical counting, rather than other methods, to ensure that the timing of movements is precise.

Group balancing and sequencing on apparatus adds an exciting array of new opportunities for transferring knowledge and safe practice learnt on the floor to creative movement development using different levels and surfaces. Pupils find ways of balancing between apparatus and partners, the floor and apparatus and different pieces of apparatus.

Once group sequences are structured and practised, the teacher engages the whole class in peer observation, inviting positive and constructive points that will continue to help improve and refine the work.

The video extracts show sensitive encouragement and extension questions from the teacher, eliciting valuable feedback comments from the observers about what they liked and why, and about ways in which further practice could help. In this feedback, the pupils identify a number of factors.

When discussing the apparatus sequences, pupils noted:

- good use of all the apparatus
- interesting use of pathways
- clarity of held balances
- good timing; counting phrases helped.

When discussing the floor sequences, pupils noted:

- good use of canon
- good sharing of space
- the use of music added to interest.

Pupils also noted, when discussing the main points for further improvement, that:

- there is room for further improvement in quality
- group work needs much practice because it relies on so many individuals
- body tension needs to be maintained to hold the shapes and stillness in the balances
- more practice would improve the flow of sequences.

Conclusion

At the end of the unit, the teacher and pupils revisit what they have learnt in the whole unit. In the example, the pupils noted that they had:

- learnt about 'taking responsibility and helping each other'
- learnt 'the importance of all roles – base and top people – in the success of group balance work'
- 'learnt new skills together'
- 'more awareness of the strength and muscle groups required for gymnastics'
- 'found ways to ensure everyone could be part of the group'

- 'thought about pathways to make the work more interesting'
- 'worked on apparatus and to music'
- appreciated 'having work cards to start ideas, then developing our own'.

Finally, we hear individual comments from three pupils about their experiences in the unit. The teacher explains the full context of the unit and the importance of gymnastics in her school.

 View video extract Unit 4 (S2).

 For suggested follow-up tasks, see page 7.

Section 2: Dimensions of Learning through Gymnastics

Dimension 1: Facilitating Learning

There are many facets to facilitating learning in and through gymnastics. For example, clarity of **communication** between teacher and pupils is essential if knowledge, skills and understanding are to develop. The greater the depth of a teacher's **knowledge and understanding**, the more confidence he/she will have to structure safe and progressive learning situations. **Planning and organisation** are essential to an environment in which risk is managed appropriately in order to provide a safe, stimulating and exciting learning environment.

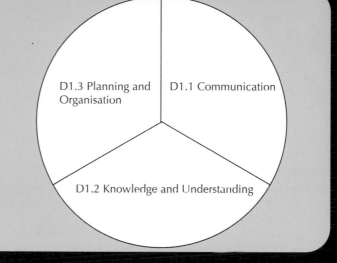

D1.3 Planning and Organisation

D1.1 Communication

D1.2 Knowledge and Understanding

D1.1 Communication

 Examples in this section of the DVD exemplify learners' engagement in acquiring linguistic and movement vocabulary. The importance of language in task-setting and teacher intervention to promote learning is also shown.

Gymnastic Vocabulary (P1 and P2)

Two video extracts illustrate development of language.

- The teacher is seen encouraging pupils to articulate what they are learning and understanding through their gymnastics experience.
- Pupils are challenged to name and demonstrate specific skills as a strategy for developing observers' movement vocabulary and knowledge.

Task-setting (S1 and P2)

- Two video extracts show clarity in the use of language in initial and developmental task setting.

 View video extract D1.1:
  - gymnastic vocabulary
  - task-setting.

 Reinforcing language through action is particularly valuable to younger pupils.

- **Succinct** use of accurate language increases time on action tasks.
- **Appropriateness** of language enables pupils to interpret words into action.

- **Clarity** in use of language (eg 'straighten your knees', 'extend your ankles') communicates most directly to improve performance.
- Encouraging pupils to **articulate** their judgements on work observed or practised, enables them to expand their gymnastic vocabulary and to engage more effectively in assessment and feedback.

 In conjunction with a school unit of work, develop a list of specific vocabulary (for example, generic actions, specific skills, movement concepts, scientific aspects of movement and the body and/or physical preparation) that the pupils need to know and understand.

D1.2 Knowledge and Understanding

Aspects of knowledge and understanding illustrated in video extracts on the DVD indicate how depth of knowledge enables teachers and pupils to facilitate developmental learning situations.

Progression in Learning (P2 and club)

The example shown is progression in the core body strength.

- The purpose of this series of video extracts on the DVD is to illustrate progressive development and use of strength in the centre of the body. This 'core strength' and stability enables more advanced skills to be performed safely and in more challenging situations.

15

Application of Knowledge (P2 and S1)

Extracts show teachers and pupils demonstrating application of knowledge.

- The teacher's knowledge is used to guide the pupils' learning through focused observation and discussion.
- Teacher and pupil improve the performance of others.

View video extract D1.2 Knowledge and Understanding, which shows:
  - progression in learning
  - application of knowledge.

Other examples of progression in learning can be seen through viewing the Synopses of Units and Dimension 5 in this handbook. The multiple aspects of progression shown on the DVD include compositional, observation and feedback skills, and understanding of physical preparation.

- Focused pupil demonstrations offer many opportunities for learning (for example, to reinforce task clarity, technical points, linking movements, quality and new ideas). Teachers and pupils apply knowledge in order to analyse what they are seeing.
- The more knowledge the teacher has about child and motor development, the science of movement (for example, kinesiology and bio-mechanics), 'moment of readiness' in skill learning, skill progressions, supports and techniques, the more help he/she can give to individuals.
- Peer mentoring develops communication skills and offers active learning opportunities for pupils to develop social skills while working cooperatively to improve the performance of others. This higher-order challenge fosters responsibility and respect between learners and develops reciprocal learning and teaching skills.

Analyse the increasing demands made on core stability and body tension in the video extract D1.2 – progressions in core body strength.

D1.3 Planning and Organisation

Whole-school schemes, units of work and lesson planning are all essential to structuring progressive, productive and enjoyable learning experiences. Links with school and local gymnastic clubs, and involvement in gymnastic festivals and competitions, all extend learning opportunities.

Whole-school Planning (P2 and S2)

- Teachers talk about gymnastics in their schools, and ways in which they have raised the profile and quality of the activity area and extended learning opportunities through school and local club links.

Lesson Structure (P1, S1 and S2)

- This series of video extracts from across the age range shows examples of lesson structure through the units of work stages of **Introduction and Physical Preparation, Development** (floor and apparatus work focusing on performance, composition and evaluation skills) and **Conclusion**, showing examples from the ends of final unit lessons where the teacher asks pupils to recall what they have learnt. There are multiple ways to plan each of these stages.

Apparatus Organisation (P1, P2 and S1)

- Pupils are seen in apparatus situations, lifting, carrying, placing and using apparatus with increasing efficiency and engagement in the decision-making process. For example, the Year 7 pupils are using apparatus plan cards, shown on the DVD, to decide who moves what to where and when.
- Multiple aspects of safety education in the management of apparatus are also essential in pupils' learning.

View video extract D1.3, showing:
  - a primary and secondary teacher talking
  - lesson structure abstracts from units of work – preparation to conclusion
  - apparatus organisation.

Well-planned apparatus layouts extend learning and provide a stimulating, challenging and imaginative environment for pupils to explore, extend their learning and enjoy.

- Safe use of apparatus involves training pupils to share responsibility for lifting and carrying, placing and using equipment, from the earliest lessons.
- Guidance on safe practice and risk-assessment, queries about placement of mats and other frequently asked questions can be found at www.afpe.org and www.british-gymnastics.org.uk

 Engage pupils in planning an apparatus layout for a specific unit of work (for example, rotation in partner work). Much can be learnt through this exercise about safe use of space and appropriateness of equipment surfaces, heights and combinations, in relation to the aim of the unit and the challenges of logistics in terms of resources and class sizes.

Dimension 2: Acquiring and Developing Skills

Movement experiences across all six of the action categories (D2.1 to D2.6) can increase movement confidence, develop a broad movement vocabulary and ensure a balanced use of the body.

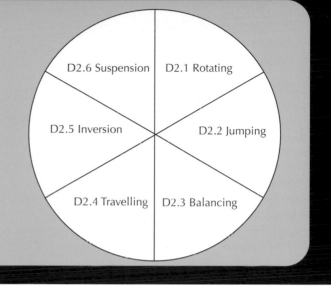

- D2.6 Suspension
- D2.1 Rotating
- D2.5 Inversion
- D2.2 Jumping
- D2.4 Travelling
- D2.3 Balancing

 The purpose of the thematic classification used here and throughout this resource is to provide the broadest possible conceptualisation of gymnastic actions. In this way, it is possible to address the needs of the widest potential audience of users of the resource, as well as to provide for pupils of all ages and abilities in the curriculum and gymnasts at all levels of experience in school and community clubs.

Providing the means for pupils of all abilities to interpret core tasks with appropriate actions and skills will help to increase the understanding of the infinite potential of the rich tapestry of gymnastic movement. By enabling creative interpretations, pupils can select, apply and justify the gymnastic vocabulary that they include in their work. At competitive levels, discrete classifications are used according to the various gymnastics disciplines, such as in Artistic Gymnastics for men and women.

In this resource, gymnastic 'actions' are defined as generic movement experiences (for example, travelling, jumping and rotating) within the thematic classification. Gymnastic 'skills' are defined as specific movement patterns that form recognisable, named elements in gymnastic vocabulary (such as the forward roll, squat vault, handstand and cartwheel).

'**Progressions**' are the building blocks in developing skilful gymnastics. Progressions involve increasing the task challenge and are best introduced to the learner 'at the moment of readiness'. Differentiated tasks can thereby cater for the individual needs of each pupil. Learning how to develop a series of actions and developmental activities that lead to the acquisition of correct techniques can offer successful and satisfying challenges to pupils as they become independent learners.

For example, progressions leading to the forward roll can begin in the Foundation Stage curriculum (children aged 3–5 years) and at Key Stage 1 (children aged 5–7 years), with body awareness actions (such as straight, tucked and straddle shapes) and, later, when learning to rock in a tucked shape on the back. This knowledge can later be incorporated into developing further progressions towards the forward roll, as exemplified on the DVD video extracts and in Section 3 (see Skill-ladder chart on page 41). The References and Further Resources section also points to British Gymnastics and other sources from which a wide range of technical information is available.

'**Technique**' is the term used in this resource to refer to the multiple components required to produce the most effective and efficient skilled performance.

The role of the teacher is to identify pupils' needs and to provide technical teaching points, in order to correct performance errors. Examples of the application of sound techniques can be found in the Skill-ladder charts in Section 3. Gymnastic techniques teaching is also extensively referenced in the References and Further Resources on the DVD-ROM, in the British Gymnastics section and in other sources.

Supporting

Physical support may be used for a number of purposes to enhance pupils' learning, including:

- ensuring safety in early attempts at a skill
- giving confidence
- guiding efforts in the right direction
- developing kinaesthetic awareness
- shaping movement pathways.

Physical contact in the form of supporting is wholly acceptable in gymnastics, provided that the pupils are aware of the need and the form the support will take.

Supporting requires a teacher to have the knowledge and experience of acceptable methods and appropriate application, according to the needs of the individual pupil. Assessment should be undertaken to determine the suitability of both the selected activity for the pupil, for example, might an alternative activity, which does not require support, be practised first? (See the British Gymnastics requirements, afPE guidance on safe practice and Child Protection in Sport Unit (CPSU) guidance on safe practice links in the References and Further Resources section on the DVD-ROM.)

When taught well, pupils who have built an extensive gymnastics movement vocabulary on floor and apparatus and have attained well-developed physical preparation can achieve high levels of independent learning and gymnastic performance.

 On the DVD, you will find either a series of linked video extracts or a montage of still images exemplifying each of the action categories of rotating, jumping, balancing, travelling, inversion and suspension. The pupils shown are aged between 8 and 14 years in curriculum gymnastics sessions, along with gymnasts from school and community clubs.

D2.1 Rotating

 There are three main **axes of rotation** in gymnastics. One is the longitudinal or vertical axis, which extends from the head to the feet, and can be used for the extended sideways or log roll, for the turning jump and for the spin on one foot. The second is the side-to-side or horizontal axis, which extends through the centre of the body from one side to the other, as seen in use in the forward roll, upward circle on a pole or by circling forward and backward between two ropes. The third is the front-to-back axis, also known as the dorsi-ventral axis as seen in the cartwheel.

D2.2 Jumping

 Learning control when **landing** from jumps onto the floor and from apparatus of increasing heights onto mats is essential to success in jumping.

- Managing a variety of **body shape**s in flight, including those with asymmetry, increases movement vocabulary and complexity.
- Developing leg strength assists with powerful and explosive **take-offs** which increase the height and extend the flight time of jumps.
- Advanced jumping skills are required to produce controlled forces in the take-offs and landings of advanced techniques, such as in vaulting and tumbling.

D2.3 Balancing

- In static balances, the mass of the body is held over the base of support, in order to show a still position.
- In dynamic balances, the mass of the body is controlled, as when moving along a narrow surface, such as a beam, the balance bar of an upturned bench or even a line on the floor. Learning 'not to wobble' is the challenge here!
- Increasing the challenge involves the pupils in progressing from balances:

  - on large bases to balances on smaller bases
  - on many bases to balances on a few bases
  - low over the base to balances high above the base
  - near to the base to balances extended away from the base
  - over a still base to balances over a moving base
  - performed singly to balances performed in sequence

© British Gymnastics

- in floor work, to balances partly on the floor and partly on apparatus, to balances entirely on apparatus
- on large and low apparatus surfaces to balances on small and high apparatus surfaces
- performed alone to balances performed with others, first without contact, then with contact, counterbalances, partial weight-taking balances and, finally, full weight-taking balances.

D2.4 Travelling

- This is defined as a transfer of body weight from one place to another by gymnastic actions, such as stepping, jumping and rolling.
- The challenge can be increased by creating complex combinations of step-patterns in composition and tumbling sequences, which involve direct linking of skills, such as rolls, cartwheels and jumps.

D2.5 Inversion

- One of the unique components of gymnastics is working 'upside-down'.
- Inversion increases vestibular awareness and experience.
- Core and upper-body strength is required to control inversion activities in which the body is supported on the hands (see video extract D1.2 for progression in core body strength).

© Volker Minkus

D2.6 Suspension

- Hanging, climbing and swinging are the gymnastic actions that make up this category.
- Apparatus is usually required in order to practise and become more skilful.
- Upper-body and hand-grip strength are needed both to hang from the apparatus by the hands, to control the swinging action and to achieve the 'pull-up' part of the climbing action.
- Leg strength and foot grip are required to achieve the 'push-up' part of the climbing action.

From Folder 1 on the DVD-ROM, select one worksheet and customise it to extend and challenge your pupils' learning.

Dimension 3: Composition

Composition is a key aspect of developing learning through gymnastics. Pupils can begin to link movements together from their first session on the floor and apparatus. The better their physical preparation and the broader their movement vocabulary, the more complex and challenging the composition work can become. Creativity, skill efficiency, musicality, fluency and variety, alongside inter-personal skills of negotiation, decision-making, communication and empathy are all challenges of the composition process.

D3.3 Increasing Complexity and Challenge

D3.1 Process

D3.2 Components

D3.1 Process

Stages of the composition process involve exploring, selecting, structuring, practising, refining and performing. These are illustrated through the following video extracts:

- P2, which shows two examples of pupils who have found linking solutions through **exploration**
- S2, which shows pupils discussing and negotiating all aspects of sequence development, including **selecting** and **structuring** of movements
- S1, which shows pupils **practising** and **refining** their work, in order to **perform** and then gain constructive peer feedback.

View video extract of the process of composition D3.1.

- Breadth of movement vocabulary is developed through many strategies, such as peer demonstration and use of visual aids.
- Finding creative responses requires confidence to 'have a go', explore and not be afraid to experience both success and failure.
- **Exploration** of movement patterns in gymnastics relates to the core action classification of rotating, jumping, travelling, balancing, inverting and suspending body weight (for example, in hanging, swinging and climbing actions).

- **Selecting** requires judgements to be made about retaining and discarding material explored in relation to the task set.
- **Structuring** requires decisions to be made about how to order material to give the greatest fluency to the sequence.
- **Practising and refining** requires time to be spent on productive repetition for the purposes of:
  - internalising movement patterns
  - enabling self-check to improve quality of performance.
- Celebrating achievement through the **performance** of sequences, in the spirit of positive, sensitive and constructive sharing, can be:
  - an essential continuation of the learning process, to give and receive feedback on strengths and areas for further refinement
  - a moment to reward effort and progress in bringing a learning experience to fruition.
- Inspiration can be gained from viewing the sequencing of movements in others' performances in, for example, festivals, televised gymnaestradas and championships, Cirque du Soleil (as illustrated on the left-hand page) and Parkour, which are all rooted in the inherent motivation and challenge of gymnastics.

Show pupils a video/DVD of a gymnastic routine/sequence video extract from the list suggested in the bullet point above and discuss what processes the gymnasts must have been through in order to achieve that level of performance.

D3.2 Components

Video extracts of key components in composition in gymnastics illustrate:

- (S2 and P1) the importance of **task clarity** in giving clear parameters for the learner to include, as appropriate, **action, spatial and dynamic content**
- (P2 and SC) attention to **continuity of movement**, with the teacher focusing on the qualities of flow and resilience to link actions or skills
- (S2 and SC) **variety in development**. Video examples show high levels of complexity in which pupils demonstrate extensive movement vocabulary, well-developed movement memory, ability to master the linking of many skills, interesting use of levels, pathways, music and multiple relationship ideas.

View video extract of composition components D3.2.

- Task-setting requires clarity in the language selected from a movement analysis framework:

- **Action concepts** (for example, rotating, jumping, travelling, balancing, inverting and hanging, swinging, climbing actions, or specific skills in those categories, such as a tuck jump, forward roll and shoulder balance)
- **Spatial concepts** (for example, shape, direction, levels and pathway)
- **Dynamic concepts** (for example, focusing attention on variations in use of time and rhythm)
- **Relationship concepts** (for example, with a partner, in a group or with apparatus).

- Tasks need to be appropriate to the stage of development of the pupils and differentiated as necessary. Younger pupils might join two rotating actions together. Older pupils might be challenged to develop group sequences with three balances and interesting changes in body shape, speed and direction and, perhaps, the use of music, which adds a further dimension to the challenge.
- **Schemes of work** in gymnastics, particularly across primary/secondary transitions, should maintain progressive movement education. This can be achieved through developing the complexity of movement analysis demands; for example, in sequencing the pupils could:
  - link two rolls
  - link two rolls that move in different directions
  - link a jump, roll and balance that show three different body shapes and a clear change of speed
  - with a partner, select four actions for the sequence, show changes of level, and use unison and canon.
- **Transitions or linking movements** within sequences need much attention. Teachers and pupils need to focus on the 'moments between', and on the qualities of fluency and resilience, as well as linking actions (such as steps, turns, twists and changes in shape or direction).
- **Variety** is a component introduced progressively as pupils develop their knowledge and understanding of movement analysis concepts and their interplay. The challenge lies in maximising the infinite 'movement palette' of action, space and dynamics and of partner, group and team learning opportunities.
- **High-quality form** in sequencing is seen where the task parameters have been met. In the sequence there is proficiency of performance, a clear start, flowing movement patterns, sustained interest, highlights in moments or phrases and a clear finish. Excellence has efficiency of movement, fluency of combination and complexity.

Set four progressive composition tasks, two on the floor and two on apparatus (with apparatus plans relevant to the specific tasks), appropriate for one of the following:

- Lower primary pupils
- Upper primary pupils
- Lower secondary pupils
- Upper secondary pupils.

D3.3 Increasing Complexity and Challenge

 The photograph montages on the DVD illustrate a range of ways in which increasing the complexity and challenges in gymnastics can be achieved. They bridge physical education, school sport and club links to add to the vision of gymnastics as a continuous and infinite area to explore.

The six montages are:

1   pupils in individual floor sequence situations
2   individual apparatus
3   pairs
4   groups
5, 6   sporting styles.

 View the six photographic montages for D3.3 – increasing complexity and challenge.

 • Task content, sequence length, use of floor and diversity of apparatus, individual, pairs, group and team sequences, vocabulary from various sporting styles, precision and control in performance and the challenge of using music all offer ways in which learning can be sustained and enhanced in the area of gymnastics.

• British Gymnastics (www.british-gymnastics.org) offers advice on further training for teachers/coaches that includes sequence/routine development, festival/schools competition possibilities and ideas.

 Observe and record an analysis of a selected gymnastics sequence or routine using the action, space and dynamics framework, with attention to relationships between gymnasts and/or apparatus.

Dimension 4: Assessment for Learning

Assessment for learning is a key professional skill for teachers. It is central to classroom practice as a means of assessing learning during lessons (formative assessment). It promotes a shared understanding of learning goals in practice and facilitates the provision of constructive guidance on ways to improve. The four characteristics of effective assessment for learning selected for exemplification and shown in the diagram opposite are among those proposed by the QCA (www.qca.org.uk).

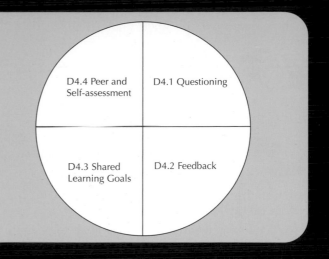

D4.4 Peer and Self-assessment | D4.1 Questioning

D4.3 Shared Learning Goals | D4.2 Feedback

D4.1 Questioning

Key points shown on the DVD video extracts relate to questions that aim to:

- facilitate continuity of learning through recall, and draw on and extend pupils' technical vocabulary of gymnastics (P1 and P2)
- confirm pupils' understanding of the purposes of the activity undertaken (S1)
- seek more advanced knowledge of physiology, enabling pupils to reveal their understanding and recall points of safety (S2)
- review aspects of safety education.

View video extract D4.1 – assessment for learning–questioning.

- Closed questions, such as 'how wide apart should the hands be in a handstand?' (Answer: 'shoulder-width…'), can help in reviewing learning experiences.
- Higher-order questions, such as 'how does getting out of breath contribute to health?', can be used to explore and extend pupils' thinking and to overcome misconceptions revealed by incorrect answers.
- Following up one answer with a further question can usefully probe pupils' knowledge and extend their learning.

Developing pupils' own questioning skills is a key aspect of their learning.

1 Find an example of higher order questioning in Unit 3 or Unit 4.

2 Go to the References and Further Resources section in Folder 3 on the DVD-ROM and to other sources for further information on developing higher-order questioning skills.

D4.2 Feedback

Feedback shown in the DVD video extracts can be used by:

- the teacher to provide immediate positive feedback and reminders of key points of technique (P2)
- pupils filming their peers to give immediate visual feedback (P2)
- the teacher to elicit from pupils both positive and developmental feedback on sequences performed in a class situation (S1)
- one pupil mentoring his partner through several progressions to achieve success (S1)
- the teacher to encourage pupils to measure their learning outcomes.

View video extract D4.2 – assessment for learning through feedback.

- Feedback related to the learning goals should be built into planning.
- Respecting pupils in the feedback given is one key to enable pupils to become confident, independent learners.

- Feedback should serve as a prompt, firstly to confirm achievement and secondly to promote development.
- Visual feedback, by way of demonstration, can be more beneficial to learners than verbal feedback.

 Teach pupils some new ways to give accurate and supportive feedback (for example, 'Well done, because you…').

D4.3 Shared Learning Goals

 The examples of sharing learning goals on the DVD video extracts show:

- the starts of two lessons in which the teacher focuses on the learning goals (P1 and P2)
- pupils setting their own learning goals to progress up the skill ladder (S1)
- safe partner balances as the focus of learning (S2).

 View video extract D4.3 – assessment for learning, shared learning goals.

 • Learning tasks developed through the lesson can be explained in the context of learning goals.

- Sharing learning goals can help pupils to appreciate the standard they should aim to achieve.
- Sharing learning goals feeds in to provision of detailed information of the assessment criteria.
- Knowing the learning goals enables pupils to select the most appropriate gymnastic movement vocabulary to fulfil tasks.

 Mentor a trainee or Higher Level Teaching Assistant, or induct a new teacher in ways of ensuring permeation of learning goals throughout a lesson.

D4.4 Peer and Self-assessment

 Pupils demonstrate their increasing ability both to reflect effectively on their own work and to observe, analyse and assess the work of others:

- One pupil observes a partner, assesses what is successful and what might be improved (P1).
- Pupils reflect at an early stage of articulating their learning experiences (P1).
- Having made an assessment, pupils suggest progressions and make changes to their peers' work to improve performance (S1 and S2).
- Having made an assessment, pupils make value judgements on the quality of their peers' performance (S2).
- Pupils report on their own learning, having assessed their progress through the unit (S2).
- A pupil reviews the learning goals in his assessment book (S1).

 View video extract D4.4 – assessment for learning – peer and self-assessment.

 • Self-assessment is a powerful tool in active learning.
• Building self-confidence is an essential ingredient in assessment practice.

- Providing a mirror wall in the teaching space can enable pupils to gain instant and ongoing opportunities to self-assess.
- Worksheets (which can be found in Folder 1 on the DVD-ROM) can be used by pupils to help them note their achievements.

 Select one of the assessment pro formas from Folder 1 of the DVD-ROM and customise it as appropriate.

Dimension 5: Extending Learning – School Sport–Club Links

This dimension focuses on a range of school and local community clubs that provide opportunities to extend learning and develop interest in the sport of gymnastics. The three styles of gymnastic discipline selected for exemplification in this resource are general gymnastics, acrobatic gymnastics and rhythmic gymnastics.

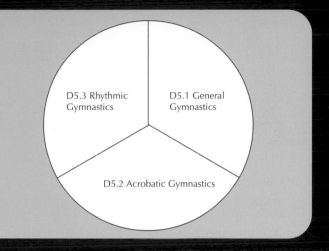

D5.3 Rhythmic Gymnastics

D5.1 General Gymnastics

D5.2 Acrobatic Gymnastics

Explanation of General Gymnastics

The term 'general gymnastics' is used here to embrace aspects from all the other styles of gymnastic discipline and is ideally suited for primary and secondary schools and community clubs. General gymnastics often includes activities rooted in floor, vault, bench and bar work, using the equipment that is most usually available in these settings. This can lead to displays, festivals, schools and inter-school competitions, or to clubs offering specific sporting styles or disciplines. The British Gymnastics disciplines are Acrobatic Gymnastics, Aerobic Gymnastics, Double Mini Tramp, General Gymnastics, Gymnastics and Movement for People with Disabilities (GMPD), Men's Artistic, Gymnastics, Rhythmic Gymnastics, Trampoline and Tumbling Gymnastics and Women's Artistic Gymnastics. British Gymnastics also offers courses and resources in pre-school gymnastics and team gym.

D5.1 General Gymnastics

School Club Team Floor

The British Schools Gymnastics Association provides many competitions for young people to participate in locally, inter-regionally and nationally. School-level competitions are provided across all gymnastic disciplines. Guidance on the judging criteria for routines is also useful for helping teachers and pupils to prepare work for festivals and displays.

Secondary School Clubs and Primary Link Clubs

The secondary school club featured on the DVD has been running for over 25 years. It provides extra-curricular gymnastics for pupils of the school and a separate **primary link club** for local feeder schools. Such provision offers a means of regular, productive engagement with others in a caring environment. Success and achievement are nurtured in this supportive and challenging extension to school life.

The head coach has led this club from the beginning and she is assisted by other qualified coaches from the local community. Some are 'home-grown', as the older gymnasts are encouraged to extend their interest and involvement into attending coach and judge education courses, thereby extending skills that they then feed back into the club.

This secondary school club provides extension-learning opportunities in floor, vault, bench, tumbling and routine work. Gymnasts can follow British Gymnastic Association proficiency awards and participate in a range of school competitions. There are active links with city clubs and some of these pupils attend both school and other local clubs. Some gymnasts move on into more discipline-specific club training situations, requiring more frequent attendance and greater commitment.

 View video extract D5.1 – extending learning – General Gymnastics.

D5.2 Acrobatic Gymnastics

School Club

The school club shown on the DVD video extracts in this section offers opportunities for secondary and primary pupils to

27

work together, predominantly in the discipline of acrobatic gymnastics. Older gymnasts are able to help the younger ones through modelling, support, and provision of one-to-one coaching. All participants make rapid progress, improving confidence, performance, knowledge, understanding and skills.

Community Club

Working in another local specialist sports college, this acrobatic and tumbling club has served the community for many years. Hundreds of young people have enjoyed the learning challenges and social benefits of belonging to such a club and many regional, national and international champions have emerged.

 View video extract D5.2 – extending learning – Acrobatic Gymnastics.

D5.3 Rhythmic Gymnastics

School Club

School clubs can provide first experiences in a range of gymnastic disciplines. In the club shown in this section, boys and girls enjoy mastering the different hand apparatus and combined body skills challenges in rhythmic gymnastics.

Community Club

Many community clubs provide further opportunities to extend learning and skill acquisition for those young people who are able and motivated to increase their training time and commitment.

Finally, talented young people demonstrate, through individual and team routines, the beauty of their sport, which they have achieved through commitment, perseverance and discipline.

View video extract D5.3 – extending learning – Rhythmic Gymnastics.

- Refer to the British Gymnastics coach education awards programmes for further information.

- See the References and Further Resources in Folder 3 on the DVD-ROM for sources of additional information to extend your knowledge, as appropriate.

Gymnastics at school, club and elite levels can offer lifelong learning opportunities, as indeed it has offered all three authors of this resource.

Voices of Participants

Coach 1 – Head Coach, School Club

'I was a physical education teacher with a strong dance and gymnastics interest, and deputy head of a school. In order to extend my knowledge, I qualified as a British Gymnastics Club Coach and have continued to update this qualification, even since retiring. Each update brings new knowledge and innovations to techniques, range and competition opportunities for school clubs. I have led this club for over 25 years as a collaborative primary/secondary schools venture and it has given me great pleasure to see the long-term development of young gymnasts into capable coaches, now nurturing the younger enthusiasts as they come to the club each week.'

Mary Small, Head Club Coach

Coach 2 – School Club

'I came to the school six years ago and am working towards gaining A Level Physical Education at the moment. Club gymnastics helps me a lot because it links with practical tests, training programmes and worksheets we have to do. I joined the club in Year 7, gradually learning new skills and entering competitions – floor and vault regional, sports acro' and aerobics, and trampolining – trying to succeed through to national level. I was encouraged to gain my Assistant Club Coach award and am currently waiting for my exam to qualify as a General Club Coach. I am also a regional judge and have helped out in a few regional competitions. I also work with the primary club – helping to put routines together for first competitions.'

Coach 3 – School Club

'I've been coming to this club since 1993 (14 years) as a participant, competitor and now as a qualified coach. I took my Assistant Club Coach award at fifteen, then the General Coach Award and started coaching here twice a week. I help out with the little ones – the primary schools' club. Now, I am a trampoline coach as well and a judge. I come to the gym club every week because I love the kids to bits; they work so hard, are very enthusiastic and they love being here.'

Gymnasts

The following is a range of responses from club participants aged 9–17 years.

Why did you join the gymnastics club?

'I was spotted at a local gymnastics festival and was invited to come along by the coach.'

'Because my coach used to teach my mum and dad…'

'I saw gymnastics on TV and thought I could be good at it, so I did some research on the Internet and found this club.'

'I saw gymnastics at the Olympics on TV and really wanted to do it.'

'I went along with my friends.'

'I joined because my sister went.'

'It helps me with my A Level Physical Education studies – to improve my grades. It's something different – I used to play football and other types of sport.'

'I like meeting new people.'

'It's fun!'

'It links between school and club very well – we do both school and club competitions. I am doing GCSE Physical Education and it helps my grades.'

'The people are very nice.'

Dimension 6: Knowledge of Health and Fitness

All gymnastic skills require a degree of strength and/or flexibility. In this respect, gymnastics is an ideal activity through which to teach an understanding of these two important elements of fitness. Specific forms of stamina are also needed in the performance and practice of gymnastics and this can easily be shown in a lesson.

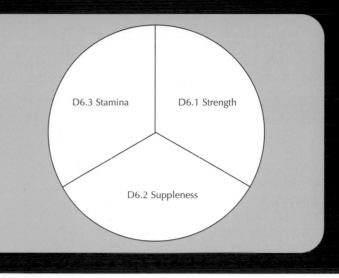

D6.1 Strength

In gymnastics, strength comes in two forms: **static strength** and **dynamic strength**. Static strength is used when a body position is held. Examples of this are the arabesque (with strong contraction of the back muscles, the buttocks and the hamstrings to hold the body line); the head stand (with tight back and abdominal muscles – good core strength – to keep the body straight); and the log roll (with strong contraction of the quadriceps and adductor muscles to keep the legs straight and tightly together).

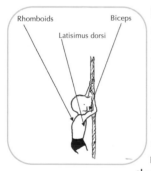

Dynamic strength is required when changing the body shape, usually to produce a force that results in movement. To propel the body into the air when jumping, the knees and ankles are straightened rapidly. The stronger the leg muscles are and the faster the legs are straightened, the higher the jump will go. In a tucked jump, the hip flexors and abdominal muscles have to work hard and fast to lift the legs quickly into the tucked shape. When climbing a rope, the Biceps, Latismus dorsi and Rhomboid muscles have to be strong to haul the weight of the body upwards and also to lower it again slowly. Regular, progressively demanding activities need practice if strength is to be developed. Climbing and physical preparation sequences (as illustrated in Section 3 of the handbook and the DVD-ROM) are good examples of how this can be done in a gymnastic setting.

D6.2 Suppleness

To achieve the correct technique and skill, the gymnast requires appropriate suppleness. For example, a handstand, which has to be held completely straight, requires flexibility in the shoulders. The free leg in the cartwheel cannot be swung far enough, or strongly enough, if the hip joints are incapable of a wide straddle. Similar flexibility is required for a good forward roll to straddle stand.

If joints are stiff because muscles are short, it can adversely affect the quality of performance. For example, a child with short, tight hamstrings will

Figure 1: Example of a physical preparation sequence

have great difficulty keeping the legs straight in a circle roll. This stiffness also makes the muscles much less efficient.

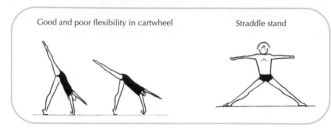

Figure 2: Examples of good and poor flexibility in the cartwheel

When muscles work, they pull and shorten. If one set of muscles is pulling to close a joint, the opposing set needs to lengthen. For example, in flexing the elbow, the biceps at the front of the upper arm shortens, and the triceps at the back of the upper arm lengthens. If one set of muscles is short, then the opposing set has to work extra hard, particularly towards the end of the action, when the joint is getting close to the end of its range. Planning advanced training in flexibility for pupils requires a depth of knowledge and experience (see the British Gymnastics Association Coach Education programme).

D6.3 Stamina

Stamina is the ability to repeat an action over a period of time. In gymnastics, having the physical resources to 'keep going' is necessary when holding a position, such as a balance, where the muscles have to remain in static contraction. This is particularly true when the balance requires considerable strength, such as in the shoulders during a handstand or the hips and abdominals in a 'V' sit. In order to refine a skill or sequence, it may well be necessary to repeat it many times. Stamina will be required in this instance if practice performance is not to suffer from the effects of fatigue. Stamina, in the form of cardio-respiratory fitness, can be developed through game activities, such as the continuous relay shown in Unit 3, which are also designed to enhance agility.

Figure 3: An example of stamina

Jumping, as in 'Examples of Physical Preparation Sequence 3' in the handbook and on the DVD-ROM, can be repeated in order to develop stamina. However, cardio-respiratory fitness can not be 'stored up'. To maintain fitness levels or to increase them, such activities as suggested here would need to be visited on a regular and frequent basis. The importance of this form of stamina, which is necessary to maintain skill levels when playing all sports, can be explained and illustrated through gymnastics.

The importance of the three elements of fitness, strength, suppleness and stamina, can clearly be exemplified while children are engaging in gymnastics. However, they will need to be shown how their own physical resources can be developed. One excellent means of doing this is through the use of physical preparation sequences (see Figure 1). These may be built up week by week as an introductory activity before the main focus of a lesson is developed. It is important to stress that, for best effect, the physical preparation sequences must be done accurately, to the fullest amplitude of performance that each individual is capable of and with control and precision. To achieve this may require additional supplementary, specific exercises to develop the required strength or suppleness. Examples of these are shown in Figures 4 and 5.

Figure 4: A back arch exercise on the floor to develop back, hip and hamstring strength for arabesque

Figure 5: Lowering into a straddle to develop side-split flexibility for forward/backward roll to straddle stand

Dimension 7: Lifelong Learning

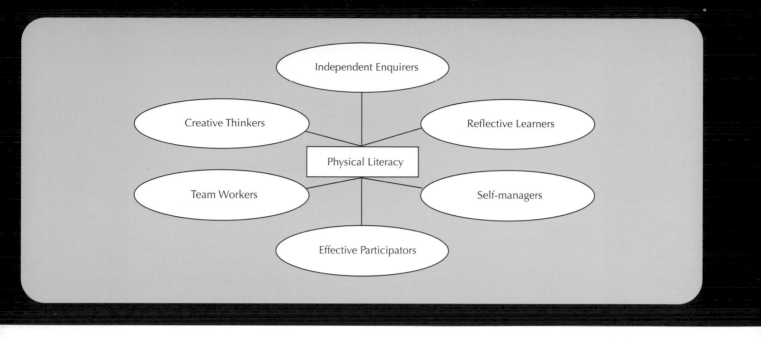

The aim of physical education is to systematically develop competence so that children are able to move efficiently, effectively and safely and understand what they are doing. The outcome – physical literacy – is as important to children's education and development as numeracy and literacy.

Margaret Talbot, Chief Executive, afPE, 2006

For this reason, the concept of physical literacy (Whitehead with Murdoch, 2006) will be at the centre of this final dimension, which encourages readers to consider how gymnastics contributes to a physical education for lifelong learning. Developing the life skill of physical literacy can be considered alongside other skills that contribute to 'success in learning, life and work', as outcomes of education making '...independent enquirers, creative thinkers, reflective learners, team workers, self-managers, effective participators'. These are the 'personal, learning and thinking skills' (PLTS) identified by the QCA (2006) that contribute to the essential skills that underpin learning and help to lay the foundations for young people to become successful learners, confident individuals and responsible citizens.

Images of young people gathered during the making of this resource and taken from the film footage, though in no great detail, and included here are intended to illustrate moments that capture the essence of these skills in action. The context of the learning in each image will be most meaningful to those who have viewed the rest of the DVD alongside this handbook. They are also intended to

stimulate curriculum debate and broaden discussion on the valuable contribution of gymnastics to quality of life and lifelong learning.

Physical Literacy

Physical literacy has been defined as the:

...motivation, confidence, physical competence, understanding and knowledge to maintain physical activity at an individually appropriate level, throughout life.

Whitehead with Murdoch, 2006

Gymnastics focuses on movement mastery, coordination, control and accuracy in movement, through developmental physical and cognitive challenges. High quality gymnastics demonstrates strength, stamina and suppleness, precision and control, efficiency and fluency in movement ability. Progressive, success-orientated learning can bring self-motivation, confidence and competence to young people. Gymnastics, then, can be seen as a potentially worthwhile activity through which young people can be nurtured in the development of physical literacy.

A framework of four key aspects of movement can be used to extend consideration of physical literacy. Ways in which these can be seen in gymnastics are described overleaf.

1 **Managing the body in relation to gravity**
Gymnastics develops work done upside-down, with body weight taken on the hands, as when performing cartwheels and handstands; work done against gravity, as when jumping and rope climbing; and when negotiating obstacles, such as vaulting over boxes.

2 **Moving in different environments**
The second strand features in most gymnastics lessons where apparatus is introduced into the environment, giving opportunities to learn how to negotiate fixed and portable obstacles.

3 **Moving in relation to fixed obstacles, manipulating objects during movement and moving in response to moving objects**
Apparatus and rhythmic gymnastics, involving the use of clubs, ropes, ribbons and hoops, requires the management of moving objects in relation to the acrobatic movements of the gymnast.

4 **Moving in relation to others**
Gymnastics offers opportunities to work in pairs and groups in creative and challenging relationships. Festivals and team competitions provide extended opportunities for collaborative work.

Personal, Learning and Thinking Skills (PLTS) (QCA, 2006)

The following descriptions of PLTS Skills are abstracted from the QCA (2006) 'A Framework of Personal, Learning and Thinking Skills' (www.qca.gov.uk).

1 **Independent enquirers** are seen as those who can process information, analyse and evaluate information, identify questions to answer and problems to resolve, explore issues from different perspectives and support conclusions using reasoned arguments and evidence.

2 **Creative thinkers** generate and explore ideas, make original connections, ask questions to extend their thinking, work with others to find imaginative solutions, try out alternatives, and adapt and follow ideas through. They also adapt ideas as circumstances change.

3 **Reflective learners** evaluate their strengths and limitations, set realistic goals with criteria for success, monitor performance and progress, invite feedback from others and make changes to further their learning. They communicate their learning in relevant ways for different purposes.

4 **Team workers** are confident and cooperative in their contribution, working with others to provide constructive help. They assume responsibility, work towards common goals and act flexibly and adapt their behaviour to suit different roles and situations.

5 **Self-managers** organise themselves, their time and their resources and show enterprise with a commitment to learning and self-improvement. They actively embrace change, anticipate, take and manage risks, cope with competing pressures and seek advice and support when needed.

6 **Effective participators** play a full part in the life of their school and actively engage in positive advocacy, bringing improvements for others, as well as themselves.

The above skills are applicable to all young people as they progress through and beyond school. Teachers and coaches play a significant part in influencing the learning experience. They also contribute to the pupils' development of positive attitudes towards sustaining lifelong learning. Gymnastics offers one exciting medium of a broad and balanced physical education and sporting experience. Gymnastics can provide exhilarating and exciting movement challenges that foster achievement, enjoyment and success.

References for Dimension 7

QCA (2006) 'A Framework of Personal, Learning and Thinking Skills'. London: QCA.

Further information is available at www.qca.gov.uk

Talbot, M. (2006) 'Response to the Keynote Article', in *Physical Education Matters*. Worcester: afPE. Vol 1: 1, p. 9.

Whitehead, M. (2005) 'Developing Physical Literacy', paper read at Roehampton University at www.physical-literacy.org.uk

Whitehead, M. with Murdoch, E. (2006) 'Physical Literacy and Physical Education: Conceptual mapping' in *Physical Education Matters*. Worcester: afPE. Vol 1: 1, pp 6–9.

Further information is available at www.physical-literacy.org.uk

Section 3: Additional Resources
Glossary

Acrobatic   Gymnastics, including tumbling, working in pairs and groups, often involving supporting others in balances.

Action   Generic movement experience applied to gymnastics (eg travelling, jumping, rotating and inverting).

Agility   The ability to change the shape of the body rapidly.

Amplitude   Maximum extension, maximum amount of space containing a movement.

Apparatus   Fixed and portable gymnastics equipment and mats.

Apparatus plan   The design of the apparatus groupings to provide a stimulating learning environment.

Arabesque   A balance on one foot, with the arms and other leg and foot extended and the body held in the horizontal plane.

Axes of rotation   Points about which the body can turn:
- horizontal axis, as in a forward roll or in circling around a horizontal bar
- longitudinal axis, as in a turning jump or a 'log' (extended sideways) roll
- dorsi-ventral (front to back) axis, as in a cartwheel.

Balance   Position of the body with the centre of mass held over the base, either when still (static) or while moving (dynamic).

Cardio-respiratory   Exercising the heart and lungs to develop an efficient oxygen transport system to feed the working muscles.

Cartwheel   An inverting, rotating and travelling action, stepping from feet to hands to feet.

Conditioning   Developing aspects of strength, flexibility and power.

Core stability   Utilisation of the abdominal and spinal muscles to provide stability, strength and control from the centre of the body.

Extend   To open the angle at a joint (eg as in straightening the knee or ankle).

Flex   To close the angle at a joint (eg as in bending the knee or ankle).

Flexibility   The range of movement at a joint.

General gymnastics   Non-specialist club activity selected from the range of gymnastics disciplines.

Gymnastics disciplines   Acrobatic Gymnastics, Aerobic Gymnastics, Double Mini Tramp, General Gymnastics, Gymnastics and Movement for People with Disabilities (GMPD), Men's Artistic, Gymnastics, Rhythmic Gymnastics, Trampoline and Tumbling Gymnastics and Women's Artistic Gymnastics Trampoline and Women's Artistic.

Inversion   Positions in which the body is upside down, usually with the head positioned lower than the hips.

Linguistic   The ability to use technical gymnastic-related vocabulary.

LTAD   Long-term Athlete Development.

Key Stage   The phases of school organisation in England.

Key Stage 2 (KS2)   Phase of school for primary school children aged 7–11 years.

Key Stage 3 (KS3)	Phase of school for secondary school children aged 11–14 years.
Moment of readiness	The appropriate time in a child's learning progression when they can attempt a more demanding task.
Peer mentor	A partner who or group that observes and analyses the performance and gives feedback.
PESSCL	The Physical Education, School Sport and Club Links strategy in England.
Pike	A gymnastic shape, like an 'L', in which there is flexion at the hips and the knees and where the ankles are held extended and together.
Progression	Moving on to a more demanding task.
Rhythmic	Gymnastics using hand apparatus, such as a ball, ribbon, hoop or clubs.
Rolling	A form of turning and rotating in which the body weight is taken successively on adjacent body parts (as in a forward roll).
Rotation	Actions in which there is a change of direction, including a turn, roll, spin, twist, jump and step.
Sequence	A series of actions combined with linking movements (transitions), which flow with continuity and control from the starting to the finishing position.
Skill	Specific movement pattern that forms an identifiable, named element in gymnastic vocabulary (eg forward roll).
Speed	The rate of transference of body weight to accelerate and decelerate.
Stamina/ endurance	The ability to sustain activity.
Straddle	A gymnastic position in which the legs are straight and wide apart.
Straight	A gymnastic shape in which the ankles, knees, hips, spine, elbows, wrists and fingers are extended and the arms are shoulder-width apart.
Strength	The maximum force that a muscle can apply.
Suppleness	The range of movement of joints.
Technique	The multiple components required to produce the most effective and efficient skilled performance.
Tension	The static contraction of the appropriate muscle in order to maintain body shape.
Tuck	A gymnastic shape in which the body joints are flexed, making a small, folded shape.
Twist	Fixing one part of the body and turning another (as in placing the hands and jumping with the feet, with a twist at the waist to the right or left, to land facing a different direction).

Skill-ladder Charts

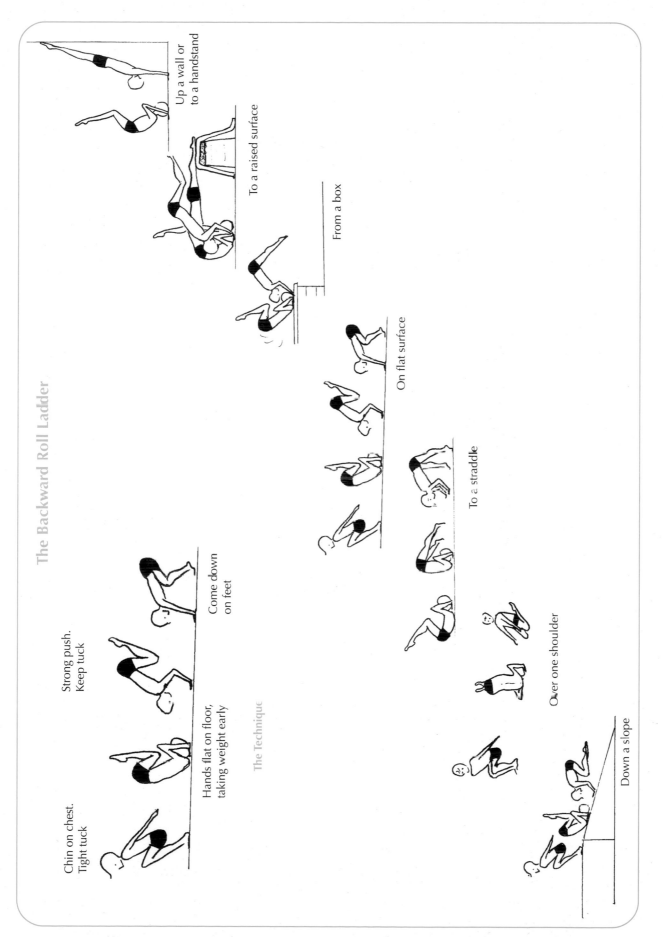

The Backward Roll Ladder

The Technique

Chin on chest.
Tight tuck

Hands flat on floor,
taking weight early

Strong push.
Keep tuck

Come down
on feet

Down a slope

Over one shoulder

To a straddle

On flat surface

From a box

To a raised surface

Up a wall or
to a handstand

The Cartwheel Ladder

One-handed

Along a bench

Over a bench

Along a line

Over a bench

Hands and feet into 'targets'

The Technique

Strong, tight finishing position

Straight legs and pointed toes. Wide straddle

Watch feet come to floor

Same hand and foot lead. Strong push from bent leg

The Support

Strongest support at mid-point of skill

Follow through with support

Take other hip as soon as possible

Reach to lead hip early

The Forward Roll Ladder

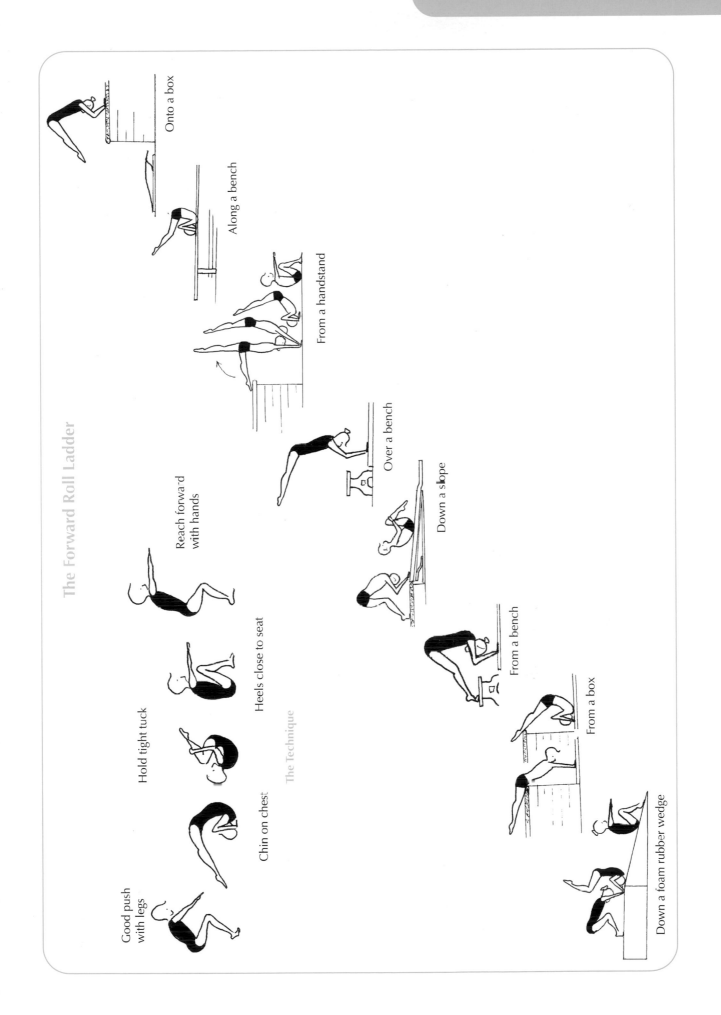

Good push with legs

Hold tight tuck

Chin on chest

Heels close to seat

Reach forward with hands

The Technique

Onto a box

Along a bench

From a handstand

Over a bench

Down a slope

From a bench

From a box

Down a foam rubber wedge

The Handstand Ladder

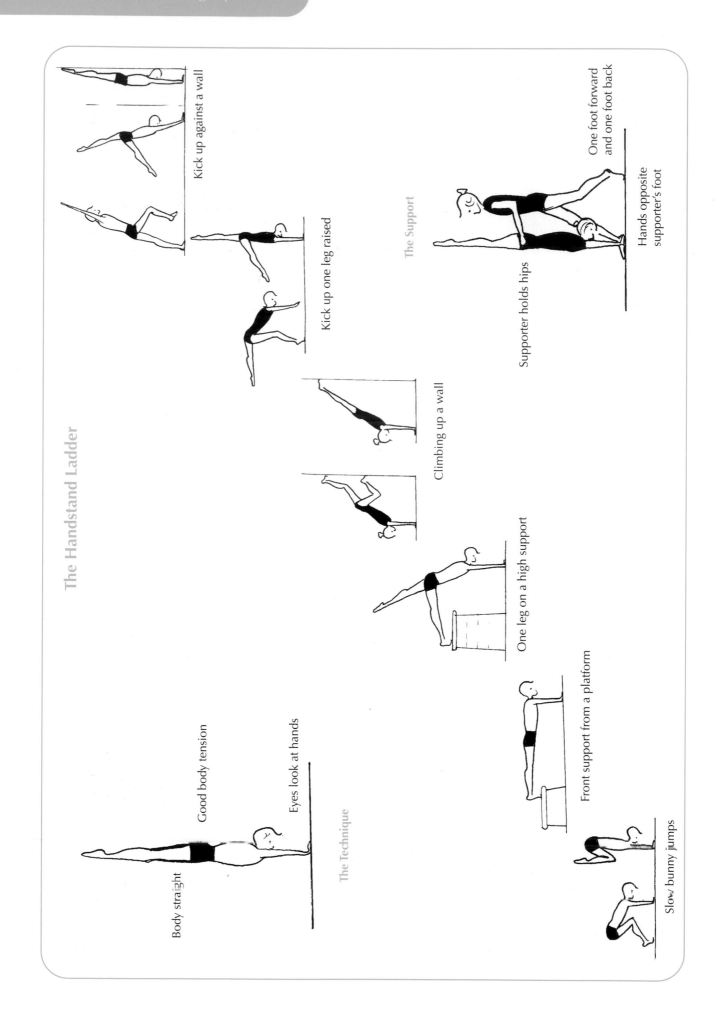

The Technique

Body straight

Good body tension

Eyes look at hands

The Support

Supporter holds hips

One foot forward and one foot back

Hands opposite supporter's foot

Kick up against a wall

Kick up one leg raised

Climbing up a wall

One leg on a high support

Front support from a platform

Slow bunny jumps

The Head Stand Ladder

In different shapes

On apparatus

The Support

Supporter holds hips

Supporter kneels down

Tucked head stand

On a box top

Against a beam/bar

Equal weight on hands and head

Good body tension

Front, top of head on floor

Hands and head form equilateral triangle

The Technique

Assisting the balance

Knees on elbows

Knees on a box top

The Jump Ladder

Strong upward swing of the arms

Body in slight dish shape

Eyes looking forward

Back flat

A good landing is quiet
Avoid deep landings

Powerful extension of knees and ankles

Land on the balls of the feet

Bend at ankles, knees and waist.
Put heels down

The Technique

From a bench or box top

Two-foot take off from floor

From a vaulting board

Rebound from a trampette

Running approach to a trampette

Different Shapes in a Jump

Pike

Straddle

Half or full

Star

Tuck

Stretch

Balance Charts

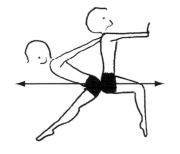

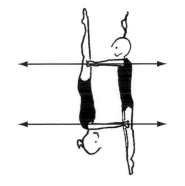

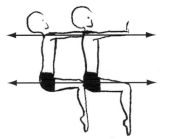

Group Balances

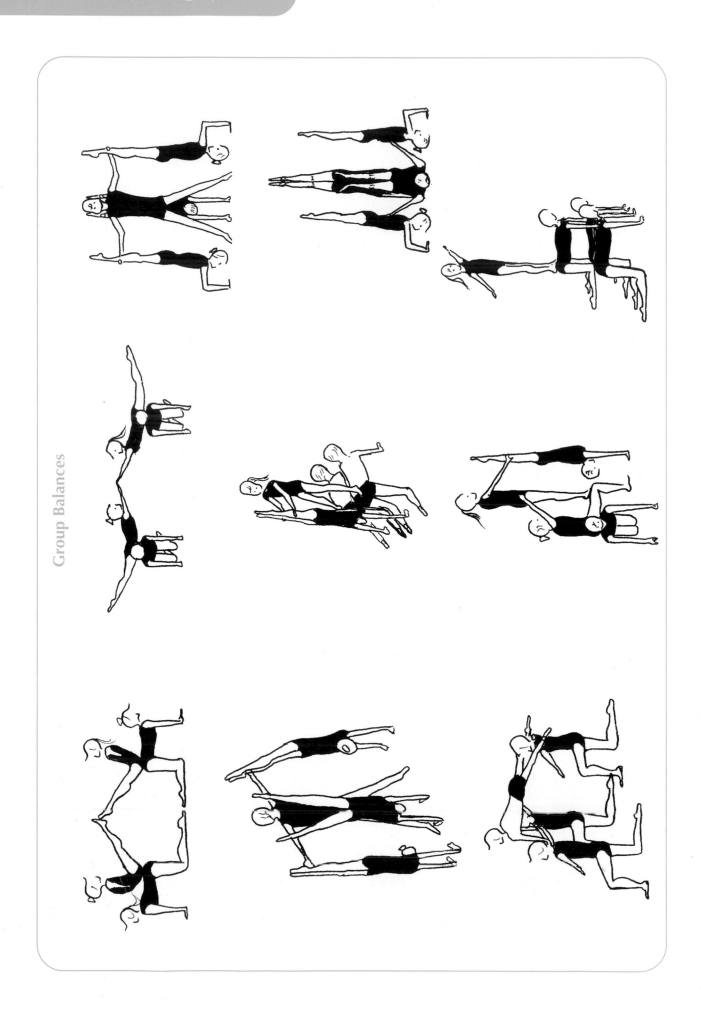

Physical Preparation Chart

Examples of Physical Preparation Sequences

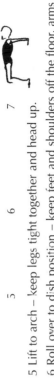

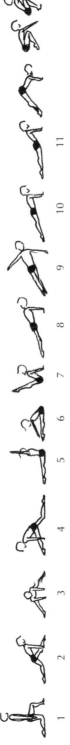

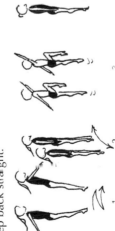

1 Arabesque. Hold a good line between hands and foot.

2 Swing the raised leg forward and make a quarter turn to a wide straddle stand.

3 Stretch forward. Keep the back straight, push the seat back and counterbalance with arms forward.

4 Put hands on the floor and walk them forward until body is fully extended and lying on the floor – keep the body, arms and legs straight.

5 Lift to arch – keep legs tight together and head up.

6 Roll over to dish position – keep feet and shoulders off the floor, arms straight, fingers just touching kneecap.

7 Lower the body to floor and push up into a bridge or crab. Each position should be held for three to five seconds.

---

1 Kneel down. Keep back straight.

2 Straighten leading leg, put hands on floor and slide front foot forward as far as possible – keep heel of back foot pointing towards the ceiling and slide forward until tension is felt in the hamstring muscle of the leading leg.

3 Turn to a straddle stand. Hands remain on floor but allow feet to slide out as far as possible.

4 Turn to splits position with other foot leading.

5 Swing back foot round to piked sit with arms raised. Keep back straight and a vertical line through hip, shoulder and hand.

6 Reach forward to piked fold. Keep back straight.

7 Rock back to supported V-sit. Legs must be straight and body folded as tightly as possible.

8 Push up to back support. Body should be straight and tight.

9 Turn to side support. Body should be tight and straight.

10 Turn to front support. Hands should be under shoulders.

11 Squat into crouch. Dip hips down and then raise seat quickly, pushing hard on floor.

12 Stand straight with good posture. Keep ankles, knees, hips and shoulders in vertical line, seat tucked in, shoulders pulled back.

A series of six jumps is illustrated. The jumps can be combined in any way to build a sequence, which could be performed to music. The length of the sequence, and thus the physical demand made, can be determined by the number of repetitions of each selected jump and the number of jumps used. All jumps should maintain quality in form and technique.

1 Jumps forward and backward, swinging arms.

2 Jumps side-to-side, with arms by side.

3 High skips on the spot with strong arm swing and ankles extended.

4 Jumping Jacks (astride jumps).

5 Change legs jumps from half-squat lunge position, with strong swing upwards of the arms and soft landing.

6 Jumps on the spot with alternate quarter turns to the left and then to the right.

User Notes for the DVD and DVD-ROM

- The DVD is compatible with versions of Word 2000 and later.
- The font used may appear inconsistent on some screens. This will depend on individual settings and may also affect the appearance of the font when printed.
- The video extracts can be viewed on most DVD players. When you load the DVD, the title screen will appear. From here, you can click to view user notes for the DVD, or choose to view the Synopses of Units of work or Dimensions of Learning through Gymnastics. By clicking on a unit, you will open the footage for that unit in the Dimension of Learning through Gymnastics, and then you can click on the different dimensions, which will open a sub-menu. By clicking on 'open' in this sub-menu, you will load the clip. At the end of each clip, you are returned to the last menu you viewed.
- You can access the additional resources of skill-ladder, balance and physical preparation charts, worksheets and list of resources, which are found on the DVD-ROM and divided between three folders, when the DVD is used in a PC. You can access the folders through My Computer, where you must right-click on the drive that your computer is reading the DVD through and click on 'open'. At this point, you will see four drives. From here, you can choose to view folders 1, 2 or 3. Double-clicking on the folder will open it up to give you access to its content.

The DVD contains:

- video extracts of synopses of units at key stages 2 and 3
- video extracts of dimension of learning 1–5.

The DVD-ROM contains:

- worksheets for you and/or your pupils to complete
- skill-ladder charts for you to print out for use with pupils
- examples of physical preparation sequences, pair and group balances
- a list of references to help you gain further information.